THE SMALL BOOK OF PRACTICAL WISDOM FOR REGULAR PEOPLE

TERRY RAY

SUNBURY PRESS

Mechanicsburg, PA USA

Published by Sunbury Press, Inc.
Mechanicsburg, Pennsylvania

www.sunburypress.com

For information about special discounts for bulk purchases, please contact Sunbury Press Orders Dept. at (855) 338-8359 or orders@sunburypress.com.

To request one of our authors for speaking engagements or book signings, please contact Sunbury Press Publicity Dept. at publicity@sunburypress.com.

ISBN: 978-1-62006-742-0 (Hard cover)

Library of Congress Number: 2016960210

FIRST SUNBURY PRESS EDITION: November 2016

Product of the United States of America
0 1 1 2 3 5 8 13 21 34 55

Set in Bookman Old Style
Designed by Crystal Devine
Cover by Lawrence Knorr
Edited by Lawrence Knorr

Continue the Enlightenment!

As the years go by
in a marriage,
the wife's circle of friends
continues to grow
while the husband's
continues to shrink
until it reaches zero.

ONE

We all live,
but there are varying degrees
of being alive.

TWO

Those who have been through
a lot in life,
but are still playful,
are a blessing to the world.

THREE

Loving someone,
and needing someone,
are two very different things.

FOUR

When you can't decide
between two things,
turn to your heart.
Its wisdom is far deeper
than that which dwells
in your head.

FIVE

The highest intellectual
accomplishment
is to do something original.

SIX

Regardless of what some men say,

the woman is always the boss of the house.

But if there are also grown daughters,

it should be noted that

'No house is big enough for two women.'

SEVEN

If a person clearly hears a question,
but responds with
'What?'
you are about to hear a lie.

EIGHT

If you are striving to achieve happiness,

always remember that,

when it comes,

it is but a passing moment.

NINE

God smiles upon His eccentric children
because they are among the few
who stop to admire
the beauty of His creation.

TEN

If you feel too tired to exercise,
more than likely
you are tired
because you are
not exercising.

ELEVEN

There is a great difference between
being you
and thinking about being you.

TWELVE

The man convinces her
he is interested
in everything she has to say.
The woman convinces him
that sexual fulfillment awaits.
And so the world turns.

THIRTEEN

Nearly all meetings are unnecessary,
but they take place
so management
can justify its existence.

FOURTEEN

People stay in marriages
for many different reasons
least of which
is love.

FIFTEEN

Raising children is very similar
to pouring concrete;
you have very little time
before the form is set.

SIXTEEN

Discussions are constructive
because there is an agreement
on the basic facts.
Arguments are destructive
because there is none.

SEVENTEEN

We do many of the same things
every day,
at the same time of the day,
but
if you derive new thoughts
and ideas
each day,
your days are meaningful.

EIGHTEEN

If you think the average person is capable

of making decisions on what is best for his own life,

then you agree with Conservatives. If you think the average person is not capable of this,

then you agree with Liberals.

NINETEEN

Only a handful
of the countless geniuses
that have walked the Earth
have been known
to the world at large.

TWENTY

If you are a person
who immediately thinks
'How can I make money on this?'
when encountering something new,
your world is very small.

TWENTY-ONE

As each generation ages,
it eventually learns
the important lessons of life
and wants to pass them on.
The succeeding generations,
in their youthful ignorance,
dismiss what they have to say.
And on it goes.

TWENTY-TWO

A democratic form of government
requires an informed electorate.
And therein lies the problem.

TWENTY-THREE

To be near the ocean,
snobs go to Martha's Vineyard
or Nantucket,
while regular people
go to Ocean City
or Virginia Beach.

TWENTY-FOUR

A Constitutional Republic
is an excellent form of government
only if
the people are courageous.

TWENTY-FIVE

It is rare to encounter a person
who has something to say
that is
unique, insightful and meaningful.

TWENTY-SIX

In dealing with
the slings and arrows of life,
mental strength is
far more important
than physical.

TWENTY-SEVEN

If you find you are more interested
in looking at yourself
in every reflective surface you
encounter
instead of the world around you,
you have a problem.

TWENTY-EIGHT

While in the universal perspective,
a human body is but
an infinitesimal speck.
But human consciousness
is as large as the universe.

TWENTY-NINE

Both history and current news
are nothing more
than opinion pieces.

THIRTY

A fundamental question of our age is
'When a woman is pregnant,
are we dealing
with one person
or two?'

THIRTY-ONE

Of all our memories,
regret
is the most difficult
to let go.

THIRTY-TWO

The passage of seasons
is the best metaphor
to understand
human life.

THIRTY-THREE

An essential question to ask yourself:
if you lose
everything you have,
would you still
be a worthy person?

THIRTY-FOUR

Most great catastrophes are caused
by the least of things.

THIRTY-FIVE

Some are in prisons
created by the state,
while most are in prisons
created by themselves.

THIRTY-SIX

There are those
who simply enjoy
watching the activities
of their children,
while there are others
who want to live
vicariously
through them.

THIRTY-SEVEN

All of our life stories are,
to some degree,
apocryphal.

THIRTY-EIGHT

It takes at least
a dozen retellings
of a story
to get the facts
just the way
you want them.

THIRTY-NINE

An apt saying
for modern day media:
'You are still a loser
if
you win the battle
but lose the war.'

FORTY

A person marooned,
alone,
on a desert island,
will still create
art.

FORTY-ONE

Nothing diminishes your self-esteem
faster
than being broke.

FORTY-TWO

Those who convince you
to be the one
to stand up against
the antagonist
will be the first to run
at the first sign
of trouble.

FORTY-THREE

There are fools who feel
that by being the loudest
in a conversation
indicates
a superior mind.

FORTY-FOUR

The force of habit
is so strong
that human beings
will continue doing
the same thing
even when they know
it will harm them.

FORTY-FIVE

Those who love to be
the bearer of bad news
are themselves
the bad news.

FORTY-SIX

Be aware of anyone
who constantly
compliments you.

FORTY-SEVEN

Tomorrow is never guaranteed.

FORTY-EIGHT

A stack of ten thousand bricks
can be easily moved
one brick at a time.

~

FORTY-NINE

Always remember that
employee loyalty
is a one way street;
while they demand it of you,
if things go bad
they will kick you to the street
in a heartbeat.

FIFTY

If you are looking for the
Elixir of Life,
spend time
watching children play.

FIFTY-ONE

If your life's goal
is to achieve perfection,
you are pursuing
the Impossible Dream.

⌒〜

FIFTY-TWO

Those who have others
depending upon them,
and still take
unnecessary risks,
are selfish people.

FIFTY-THREE

If you lead a life
where something is new
every day,
you are blessed.

FIFTY-FOUR

Many of the people you envy
wish they were you.

FIFTY-FIVE

If you feel
your life
is one problem
after another,
you are living
a normal life.

FIFTY-SIX

If you have discovered
that love is the fabric of the universe,
you have found
wisdom.

FIFTY-SEVEN

Live your life

in an honorable, reasonable and honest way.

If there are some

who criticize you,

pay no more attention to them

than you would

an off-key musician.

FIFTY-EIGHT

Better to die at twenty,
having lived a full life,
than die at ninety,
having never lived at all.

FIFTY-NINE

Among the advantages of growing old
is the significant amount of time
to do meaningful things
that was once wasted
looking for sex.

SIXTY

Under any given circumstance,
all of us have the potential
of either rising to heroism
or succumbing to cowardice.

SIXTY-ONE

Life after death
will be dependent upon
whether our self-awareness
is a physical part of our body
or something
separate from it.

SIXTY-TWO

If a man is arrested for rape,
a lawyer will either passionately argue
for his innocence
or for his guilt
depending upon
whether the man
or the woman
gets to his office first.

SIXTY-THREE

A politician is a chameleon
who can become
anyone
under any given circumstance.

SIXTY-FOUR

Professors spend most of their lives
cloistered behind the protective walls
of the Ivory Tower
so they can become certified
to teach young students
about real life.

SIXTY-FIVE

The only truly effective way
to cope with heartbreak
is travel.

SIXTY-SIX

Seeking fame
is wanting people
you don't know,
and who don't know you,
to adore you.

SIXTY-SEVEN

Those who heap praise
upon themselves
feel the opposite way
about themselves.

SIXTY-EIGHT

There is an infinitely large universe
surrounding us
and an infinitely small universe
inside us.
Both of these universes
are the same thing.

SIXTY-NINE

The older you get,
the more the significance
of the ordinary problems of life
shrinks in proportion.

SEVENTY

Always remember that
when you meet someone,
it is only a snapshot
of an ever-changing life,
that will be different in a year,
much different in five,
and entirely different in ten.

SEVENTY-ONE

Perfection lies only with God.

SEVENTY-TWO

Those who believe
that the end justifies the means
are sailing a ship
without a compass.

SEVENTY-THREE

Many discover afterwards
that it wasn't your ex-spouse,
but
that you just weren't cut out
for marriage
itself.

SEVENTY-FOUR

If you want a relationship that lasts,
look for someone
who has a great sense of humor
and loves to laugh.

SEVENTY-FIVE

Bad spelling
and grammar
appear to have become
the norm.

SEVENTY-SIX

Admitting defeat
is sometimes
the path of wisdom.

SEVENTY-SEVEN

If you often help others
and expect they would
do the same for you,
you are in
for a big disappointment.

SEVENTY-EIGHT

Manners are the foundation
for civilized behavior;
civilization
is in bad shape.

SEVENTY-NINE

If you enjoy meeting strangers,
look in the mirror.

EIGHTY

A very old man spends every day
on his porch rocker
watching life go by.
A young ambitious man asks him,
'What is the purpose of your life?'
the old man replies,
'What is the purpose of yours?'

EIGHTY-ONE

Anytime a country loses
its vitality, strength and courage,
there will be barbarians at the gate
ready to replace it.

EIGHTY-TWO

Be joyful
that life is a mystery.
How tedious our lives would be
if we already knew
the outcome of the story.

EIGHTY-THREE

Some ask,
'What is he worth?'
If the answer is
in terms of his possessions,
he is a very poor man
indeed.

EIGHTY-FOUR

The vanishing pleasure
of actually speaking
with another human being
gives presage
to the decline
of our humanity.

EIGHTY-FIVE

If intelligent beings from another planet
made an appearance on Earth,
the animosities we have
among ourselves
would disappear.

EIGHTY-SIX

I never spoke to my neighbor,
but saw him on a country road
and tipped my hat,
then saw him in another city
and shook his hand,
then saw him in another country
and embraced him.

EIGHTY-SEVEN

Those who expect that
equality among all people
will someday become a reality
are destined
for great disappointment.

EIGHTY-EIGHT

Among the great variety of snobs,
art snobs are among the most
repelling.

EIGHTY-NINE

Never miss a moment of joy
when your children are small,
because,
if you blink,
they no longer are.

NINETY

Some wish for a perfect memory
so nothing is forgotten.
But God gave us faulty recollection
as His way of protecting us
from the horror and grief
in our past.

NINETY-ONE

Earthlike planets are constantly discovered.

We can't imagine what the beings are like.

But, one thing we surely have in common

is pondering of why we exist.

NINETY-TWO

Being a parent
is the most difficult and important job
anyone ever undertakes,
and the results
are always
completely unpredictable.

NINETY-THREE

What you come to realize
as you age
is that those silly things
you did as a child
were the best times
of your life.

NINETY-FOUR

One of life's great ironies
is that what first
attracted you to someone
is sometimes
the same thing
that eventually
pushes you apart.

NINETY-FIVE

Life is meant to be lived,
not just watched.

NINETY-SIX

Like shopping for shoes,
much of life is spent
searching for what
you think you like
then seeing
if it fits.

NINETY-SEVEN

Those who have
a mission in life
are blessed.

NINETY-EIGHT

There are times
when the truth is abhorred
and the lie
adored.

NINETY-NINE

The never-faltering love
you see
in your dog's eyes
is a small peek
into heaven.

ONE HUNDRED